Welcome ab  Anthology

Published in 2000 by New Departures
PO Box 9819, London W11 2GQ

A CIP catalogue record for this book is available from the British Library.

The **POP !** Anthology   (New Departures 25—26)
Edited by Michael Horovitz and Inge Elsa Laird

ISBN 0 902689 19 3

One Pound from each copy of this book sold will be donated to the Hackney Children's Hospital.

This book was designed by 2nd Year students from BA Graphic
and Media Design (Typography) at the London College of Printing.

Project Coordinator: Joe Paice

Design Initiation: Ian Noble

Cover Design and Layout: Markus Obladen

Project Assistant: Tammy Stone

Design Team: Kristoffer Busch

     Maro Kakari

     David Kendall

     Graham Mansfield

     Claes Morén

     Karin Ödin

     Anna Sjöstrand

     Jeanette Söderqvist

     Christoph Stolberg

     Martin Vowles

Printed by: Sterling

Paper supplied by: Robert Horne

Design

Contents

OLYMPIC INVOCATION

TUNE IN

Not a poetry picnic for the bards to enthral
But Poetry Olympics at the Festival Hall
The only Metres run will be the metre of line
The only High Jump they'll get is if they run over time

    AND SWITCH OVER

    And a man like a bomb flies down the wing
      – flies down the wing
    On a wing and a prayer
    Tiptoes through the lions' lair
    Cuts through the defence, decimates the attack
    Scores a goal. "Pure Poetry," Jimmy Hill growls.

SWITCH BACK

And a weatherman (a closet poet if ever there was one)
Performs his piece, words swill as arm sweeps:
"Sweeping rain and a quiet mist
A touch of thunder will pass in the night
And the blackened ice will melt by morning light."

    SWITCH OVER

    And an advert broadcasts a poet in a wheelchair
    John Betjeman catches the wind in his hair.
    Asked if he had any regrets
    "Yes," he said, "Not enough sex."

ming couplets ring to entice — it's
try in adverts and we don't realise
s in birthday cards, in the papers every week
s poetry we think and imperfectly speak —

    It's poetry on gravestones, in nursery rhymes
    Poetry documentaries that document the times
    It's poetry on buses and poems on the tubes
    And in the printed matter, whether it matters or not to you
    It's poems in the prayer-books and on protest marches
    Poetry sprayed in aerosol underneath the arches.

ll out - tune in as they might have said:
try is life - without it you're dead.

Among the writers and performers represented in this book:–

Top: Joe Strummer, Keith Waithe, Jean 'Binta' Breeze, Ifigenija Simonovic, Beryl Bainbridge, Allen Ginsberg, Grace Nichols, Adrian Mitchell, Ernst Jandl, Carol Ann Duffy, Adam Horovitz, Ian Dury, Hanif Kureishi, Inge Elsa Laird, Günter Grass, Ted Hughes, Valerie Bloom

Middle: Seamus Heaney, John Agard, Ruth Vaughn, Frieda Hughes, Stephen Spender, Claire Calman, Samuel Beckett, Stan Tracey, Paul Weller, William Burroughs

Bottom: Julie Felix, Jack Kerouac, Damon Albarn, Mahmood Jamal, Libby Houston, Linton Kwesi Johnson, Kirsty MacColl, John Hegley, Fran Landesman, Patience Agbabi, R D Laing, Thom Gunn, Brian Patten, Christopher Logue, Jill Neville, Michael Horovitz, Harry Fainlight, Kathleen Raine, Frances Horovitz, Stevie Smith

POP!

Salutations, Keynotes, Reaffirmations
– *beyond the Mercenary Nillennium*

Michael Horovitz

Soon after Anna Lovell, David Sladen and I had founded *New Departures* at Oxford in the summer of 1959, David took a teaching post in Teheran and used the first issue to help his students learn English. One of them translated the magazine's name into the Persian for 'New Deaths'!

Forty-one years and a mounting multitude of deaths later, the platform itself survives, enabling further departures and apparently unfashionable transports toward the Healing of Nations aspired to by our Poetry Olympics festivals.

This issue doubles as a reunion-and-continuity confluence at the turn of the century, and as a hymn book-cum-programme for my 65th birthday party at London's Royal Festival Hall on Tuesday 4th April 2000.

In June 1965 the Royal Albert Hall was filled to overflowing for world poetry. By the autumn of 1980 a creeping careerist Little England dullness had set in again, trying to keep literary culture fenced into a game reserve in thrall to the xenophobic conformities of Philip Larkin, Kingsley Amis and their acolytes.

Thom Gunn among others has pointed out that ". . . The trouble is the English are hung up on Larkin . . . Right now he exercises a terrible influence on English poetry because if you admire somebody like that so much it means you're not going to be aiming very high." (*Shelf Life*, Faber 1989)

When on top of this Margaret Thatcher tried to boycott British athletes from participating in the 1980 Moscow Olympics, my friends and I felt it was high time we tried to restore the pure-spirited pursuit of artistic excellence which had planted literature and the arts at the heart of the original Olympics.

As Ted Hughes wrote in a manifesto for our Westminster Abbey launch, " . . .The idea of global unity is not new, but the absolute necessity of it has only just arrived, like a sudden radical alteration of the sun, and we shall have to adapt or disappear." (*New Departures 12*, 1980)

I was the youngest of ten children whose parents brought us from Nazi Germany to England in 1937. For most of the Second World War years our network of refugee families moved precariously between various temporary homes around London, the Home Counties and the Thames Valley. The informal village entertainments we presented for all comers

weekends and holidays, featuring readings, songs, clowning, drama
ıd music, seem to have sown the seeds of my later preoccupation
th arts circuses and road shows.

And the artists, writers, troubadours and musicians in the 'Live
ew Departures', Jazz Poetry SuperJam and Poetry Olympics
ındwagons, gradually became my adopted family. This collection
cludes memories of and revisitations to some of the many pioneers
ho were kind enough to adopt me in turn: the perennial lighthouse
ıat is Samuel Beckett; the still unsung maestro of both music and
erse, Moondog, who gave his last performance in Britain at our 1996
)W! Festival at the Albert Hall; "Blake's purest daughter", the resonant
evie Smith; dear departed beat prophets Kerouac, Ginsberg and
ırroughs; R D Laing, Stephen Spender, Ted Hughes and several
milarly passionate and dedicated younger poets who died long before
eir time – Frances Horovitz, Harry Fainlight, Jill Neville.

And now, just eight days before he was poised to spread his
imitable POP'n'rockular songwings at our bardic regeneration gig, Ian
ury, poet laureate of mockney blisspunk, has left us for the music
ılls of Elysium. " – *What a lovely bloke*", as Paul McCartney says in a
essage sent specially for this book: " . . . *He hit me with his loving.*"
s he did so many, and will long go on doing, for anyone who hears a
cording, or bears his generous spirit in mind.

s reassuring to hand on the time-travelling baton of art by ventilating
jain, from New Departures 1975, something closer to line-by-line
ersification than anything else I've seen by William Burroughs; to
kindle the flame of living tradition and of honour among poets
ticulated by *hommages* like that of Patience Agbabi's tattooing poem
ı Thom Gunn's of 40 years before – and by Seamus Heaney's poignant
egy for his friend Joseph Brodsky, in the identical mesmerising metre
ıd lilting gravitas with which Auden mourned W B Yeats 60 years ago.

The high level overlaps between poetry and song, and
etween poetry in performance and stand-up comedy, are celebrated
ıd extended in these pages – as is the social and political commitment
f such uncompromising voices against injustice as Valerie Bloom,
nton Kwesi Johnson and Mahmood Jamal. (Readers unguarded against
ıe insidious virus of hypertitis should be warned that Linton's *Di
ınfinish Revalueshan* predates, and bears no connection with, the arch-
lairite Philip Gould's *Unfinished Revolution: How the Modernisers saved
ıe Labour Party*. This sell-out of socialism to the Big Lies of PR might
egin to comply with any meaningful yardstick of 'fair trading'
ınguage by retitling itself 'The *Unstarted* Revolution'.)

The poem *Words* which Stevie Smith gave me for New
epartures 1 has not, as far as I've noticed, subsequently reappeared

anywhere else. Its theme ("*Can it be that the tongue is cursed, to go so wrong?*") remains chillingly contemporary, given the unabating pile-up of abuses of language and behaviour, worldwide. More and more politicians are apparently bent on little more than garnering loadsamoney, and living out John Steinbeck's definition: "A politician is someone who approaches every problem with an open mouth". They, and we, would do better to reflect, with Stevie and Wittgenstein, on the stimulating difficulties of attempting to improve on a blank sheet of paper.

At a retirement age birthday, reconsideration of origins and of destinations is as fitting as the troops of friends and relations. If these decades of presenting more communicative poetry and music on page and stage, in the air and on aural record, have raised consciousness and given pleasure, well and good. If popular songwriting and singing have improved, and pop artists added to the gaiety of nations, whilst diminishing their military, territorial and competitively industrial ambitions, even better.

And best of all if our impulses and productions, including this word, picture and sound-hoard, are understood to be making a *genuine* difference, at the ludicrously overblown Nillennium across these polluted shores of only –more–of–the–same – that's to say, of heartless iron-arsed Thatcherite wage slavery, exploitation, greed and Rule-of-bank balance and commerce, sanctioned by brute force.

With birth, inner growth and rebirth in mind, I'm sealing this bran-tub of a few of my favourite things with a garland of thank-yous to my parents and siblings; most notably to my mother, who died – aged one hundred years and eight months – as she had lived, in inspired and inspiring harmony with her angels. Despite exceedingly harsh circumstances from the mid-1930s on, she gave her children a marvellous start and a unique drive in life. Something of the spirit of it might be sensed from the snapshot reproduced on page 118, of my younger sibs and me at croquet during our last months of residential ease in that Frankfurt garden.

Special ambrosiac champagne buckets of thanks are due to Inge Elsa Laird, long-serving coeditor and buddy way beyond the calls of love or duty; to David Russell, secretarial saint; to Lynne Sims, Mick Freed, Julian Mason and Jeremy Scott, and to Joe Paice and the team of design and typography students at the London College of Printing, for their patient, unstinting and infinitely resourceful transpositions of the erratic flurries of difficult texts we've been showering them with day and night. And further thanks to the hundreds of fellow artists, writers and friends of radical arts movements, without whose support this miscellany and festival – like their predecessors – could not have been put together so substantially.

Kathleen Raine wrote at the outset of Poetry Olympics in 1980:

". . . I do believe, as you do, that the world can be saved – or that human beings can be saved from the world – only by the Imagination, which, whether in poetry and the other arts, or in life itself, is the expression of our true humanity. You and I are both in our way trying to make effective the teaching of Blake, that Imagination is "the human nature itself" and that works of Imagination are the language in which members of every race in every period of the past, present and future, can understand and communicate with one another."

Ted Hughes echoed this, for the same occasion: ". . . If the various nations are ever to make a working synthesis of their fierce contradictions, the plan of it and the temper of it will be created in spirit before it can be formulated or accepted in political fact. And it is in poetry that we can refresh our hope that such a unity is occupying people's imaginations everywhere, since poetry is the voice of spirit and imagination and all that is potential, as well as of the healing benevolence that used to be the privilege of the gods."

The poem Ted contributed for the launch of Poetry Olympics stands as true and as resolute as ever, at this turn of the century: —

THE WORD RIVER

Fallen from heaven, lies across
The lap of his mother, broken by world.

But the river cannot be killed, whatever.
It goes on, flowing from heaven,

In dumbness uttering spirit brightness
Through its broken mouth.

Broken in a million pieces and buried
Its dry tomb will split, at a sign in the sky,

At a rending of veils.
It will rise, in a time after times,

After swallowing death and the pit
It will return stainless

For the delivery of this world.
So the river is a god

Knee-deep among reeds, watching men,
Or hung by the heels down the cascades of a dam

It is a god, and inviolable.
Immortal. And it will wash itself of our deaths.

Second Day at Lumb Bank (Pages 58 to 59):
Lumb Bank is the West Yorkshire estate Ted Hughes made over to house one of t
Arvon Foundation Writing Centres, at which Frances was always much in deman
setting the highest of standards for the tricky job of tutoring would-be poets. T
second day of each course is set aside for field work.

TO BE HARRY (P 67):
Ted Hughes wrote this poem in the late autumn of 1982, when I asked if he wou
contribute to a Harry Fainlight memorial section I was putting together in N
Departures 14. Harry had been found dead of bronchial pneumonia outside h
remote cottage in Wales only a few days before.

In my haste to get the issue printed, I overlooked a factual error Ted had made
his otherwise perfectly pitched requiem. To wit – it was not *Oz* magazine, but
(*International Times*), in whose staged death and resurrection Harry played t
body role in the spring of 1967.

IT had swiftly become, as Jonathon Green remarks in the 'Underground Pres
chapter of his *All Dressed Up* (Cape 1998), ". . . the counter-culture's fortnightly
choice". Its headquarters suffered a mammoth police raid on 9 March at the end
which everything in the entire office was seized, and kept for two months.

Green recalls that ". . . On 11 March the paper staged 'The Death of *IT*', a piece
street theatre that focused on a small march down Whitehall to the Cenotaph, muc
revered memorial to the dead of two world wars. Here, as the thirty-odd weirdly-dress
beatniks and their girlfriends looked on, Harry Fainlight, of Albert Hall poetry readi
fame, climbed into a scarlet coffin. Chanting began and daffodils were piled on to th
recumbent poet.

"The police appeared and the group moved on, taking the coffin to Westminst
Underground station where the crowd began four hours of travelling round the Circ
Line, still chanting, playing flutes, guitars and bongos. Only after the LT police thre
them off did the procession reemerge, at Notting Hill, to march down Portobello Roa
coffin shouldered, instruments blaring on.

"The tabloids reacted as required. The *Sunday Mirror*'s man, quitting El Vino's for th
occasion to write as '14182973 Lance-Corporal Geoffrey Ross', was especially incense
and talked of a 'Cenotaph Sacrilege'. Surprisingly he recanted somewhat a week late
after a letter from Mick Farren, foremost among the marchers, noted that his own fath
had died during the Second World War and that if alternative views could not be voice
what had been the point of the whole 'struggle for democracy'?"

ART WORKS

Self Portrait as Poetry Olympics Torchbearer by Michael Horovitz c. 1970

6 Lightning stamp, (c) The Post Office 2000

7 Chicken/Egg cartoon by B P, from *The Spectator Cartoon Book 1999*, ed. Michael Heath, Profile Books/The Spectator 1999

8 Mel Calman cartoons from *My God* (Souvenir Press 1970), (c) S & C Calman

2 *Photomontage of John Lennon 1940 – 1980* made by Peter Blake on 14/2/81 for the cover of New Departures 13,1981

3 *The Virgin Punishing the Infant Jesus* by Max Ernst, 1926

6 Bike stamp (c) The Post Office 2000

7 *Praying Jew (Jew in Black and White)* by Marc Chagall, 1914

4 Drawings for Günter Grass's poems in *New Departures 15* by Ron Sandford, 982

7 Painting of *W B Yeats* by John Butler Yeats the Elder, c. 1900, courtesy National Gallery of Ireland; Drawing of *W H Auden* by David Hockney, 1969

2 Photo-collage of *Stephen Spender* by David Hockney, 1985

9 Waterfall drawing by Jane Percival, made for *New Departures 5*, 1970

0 *Pigs at Blair's money-trough* cartoon by Nicola Jennings, made for The Guardian of 4/2/99, with Stephen Byers's declaration that "Wealth creation is more important than wealth distribution" in mind (Mansion House speech, 2 February 999)

1 *Christ driving the Traders from the Temple* by El Greco c. 1600 (El Greco made at least five paintings of the subject. This version is reproduced courtesy of the National Gallery, London)

7 Road stamp, (c) The Post Office 2000

5 Tory Blair cartoon by Peter Brookes, (c) Peter Brookes/Times Newspapers Ltd, 4 March 1995; New Lab-Con Alliance cartoon by Steve Bell for the Guardian, 20 anuary, 1999

0 Louis Armstrong photomontage by Tammy Stone/Joe Paice, 2000

00 Portrait of Stevie Smith by John Furnival, c. 1981

01 Portrait of William Blake by John Linnell, 1820

02 Engraving of moon-ark and dove of peace from Bryant's *Mythology*, 1774 – 776, probably by Blake

03 Moon-ark from William Blake's *Jerusalem*, 1804 – 1820

06 Crayon drawing *Worldly Ear* by Stevie Smith, probably early 1960s

09 Drawing of *Stephen Spender on the Wuxi Shanghai Express* by David Hockney, 981

16 *Self-Portrait with Joshua on Bicycle* by Ruth Vaughn 1999

22 Sketch of *Rosi Horovitz* by Michael Horovitz, 1987

24 Drawings of *Rosi on her Deathbed* by M H, 26 May 1995

ACKNOWLEDGEMENTS

inside front cover *Party* and *A Jazz Poem?* by Paul Weller appeared in *New Departures 14*, 1982

1 Ted Hughes contributed THE WORD RIVER to *New Departures 12*, 1980

6 Excerpt from *The Gift of Flame*, which was written for the Royal Mail stamps, *Fire and Light*, February 2000

7 John Agard's *Prayer to Laughter* comes from *Laughter is an Egg* (Viking 1990)

8 *If* comes from Patience Agbabi's *Transformatrix* (Payback Press 2000)

21 *i m Samuel Beckett* appears in Michael Horovitz's *Wordsounds & Sightlines: New and Selected Poems* (Sinclair Stevenson 1994)

22 *something there* by Samuel Beckett was first published in New Departures 7/8 + 10/11 (BIG HUGE), 1975, then included in *Collected Poems* (Calder 1984)

23 Beckett sent *PSS* for *New Departures 14*, 1982

26 William Burroughs contributed *The Evening News* to the *BIG HUGE New Departures*, 1975

Acknowledgements

32 Carol Ann Duffy's *Liverpool Echo* comes from *Standing Female Nude* (Anvil Press Poetry 1985)

33 Duffy's *Virgin Punishing the Infant* is in *Selling Manhattan* (Anvil 1987)

34 Ian Dury's *GERALDINE* is reproduced courtesy of Mute Song Ltd, as is his *BED O' ROSES No 9* on p 35; both songs can be heard in his fruity staccato on his last album with the Blockheads, *Mr. Love Pants* (Ronnie Harris Records 1998)

36 Carol Ann Duffy's *– –/ –/99* was written on commission for the Salisbury Festival's 1999 Last Words project, and published in the anthology *Last Words: New Poetry for the New Century* (Picador / Macmillan1999)

37 Harry Fainlight's *July 1959* was published in his posthumous *Selected Poems*, edited by Ruth Fainlight, as were *Fugue* on p 38 and *The Jew* on p 39 (Turret Books 1986)

40 Julie Felix's *Sappho* is on her *Bright Shadows* cassette, available from Remarkable Records, http://www.remarkable.freeserve.co.uk – and 201 Town St, Middleton, Leeds LS10 3SN

42 Allen Ginsberg gave me *Mandala* for New Departures 2/3, 1960; *Returning to the Country for a Brief Visit* was in the *BIG HUGE* New Departures 1975; *Maturity* comes from *White Shroud: Poems 1980 – 85* (Viking 1987)

43 Ginsberg's *After Lalon* is in *Cosmopolitan Greetings* (Penguin 1994)

44 Günter Grass's poems, translated by John Fisher, come from *New Departures 15*, 1983

44 Thom Gunn's *Blackie, the Electric Rembrandt* comes from *My Sad Captains*, Faber 1961

47 *Audenesque* by Seamus Heaney was first published in the *TLS*, 9 February 1996

53 A different version of David Hockney's memoir of Stephen Spender appeared in *The Sunday Times* BOOKS Section on 23 July 1995

55 The hand written poem *Riddle* by Frances Horovitz first appeared in *New Departures 16: A Celebration of & for Frances Horovitz (1938 – 1983)*, 1984

56 *Letter to my Son* is included in Frances's *Collected Poems* (Bloodaxe Books, 1985)

58 *Second Day at Lumb Bank* was first published in *Singing Brink: an Anthology of Poetry from Lumb Bank*, edited by Maura Dooley and David Hunter (Arvon Press 1987)

60 *A New Waste Land* by Michael Horovitz is *New Departures 27 – 29*, 2000

62 *A Thanks, for Allen Ginsberg* by Libby Houston is in *Cover of Darkness: Selected Poems 1961 – 1998* (Slow Dancer Press 1999)

63 *Caesarian* by Frieda Hughes comes from *Wooroloo* (Bloodaxe Books 1999), as does *Readers* on p 64

66 Ted Hughes gave me *Beware of the Stars* for New Departures 1975, as he did *TO BE HARRY* on p 67, for *New Departures 15*, 1983

68 Ted's *Full Moon and Little Frieda* is in *Wodwo* (Faber and Faber 1982)

69 *For Ted Hughes* by John Agard first appeared in *Poetry Review* (Winter 1998/9)

70 *Di Anfinish Revalueshan* is in Linton Kwesi Johnson's *Tings an Times: Selected Poems* (Bloodaxe 1991), and on the *Grandchildren of Albion Live* CD & cassette

74 *Pain through Friction (frau)* by Ernst Jandl first appeared in *Wholly Communion* (Lorrimer Films 1965), the book of the film of the First International Poetry Incarnation at Albert Hall, London. Both book and video are available via Hathor Publishing, fax (01536) 790505

75 "I clearly saw . . ." by Jack Kerouac first appeared in *New Departures 2/3*, 1960

78 R D Laing's two poems were published in *New Departures 12*, 1980

79 Part 1 of Inge Elsa Laird's *THE STATE* appeared in *New Departures 15*, 1983, along with its German original

80 *Are you Satisfied ?* and also *Deeply Shallow* on p 81, are in Fran Landesman's *Rhymes at Midnight* (Golden Handshake 1996)

82 You can hear *White Nightmare* chanted by Fran, accompanied by her singer-guitarist son Miles, on the first *Poetry Olmypics* album (All Round Records ARRLP 1, 1982)

84 *I Shall Vote Labour* comes from Christopher Logue's *Selected Poems* (Faber 1996)

86 Damon Albarn's *On Your Own* is on the album *blur* of 1997, (c) EMI Publishing 1997

87 *Autumngirlsoup* by Kirsty MacColl is (c) 1999 Ocean Songs Ltd/Chrysalis Music Ltd

14

hirley Manson's *Hammering in my Head* is on Garbage's *Version 2.0* (Mushroom
rds 1998), (c) 1998 Rondor Music for the World Ltd
he Belgian Ernst Moermann's *Louis Armstrong* first appeared in Beckett's
slation in Nancy Cunard's anthology *Negro* (Paris,1934)
drian Mitchell's *Nine Ways of Looking at Ted Hughes* are in *The Epic Poise: A
bration of Ted Hughes* edited by Dick Gammage (Faber and Faber 1999)
drian's *Moondog* is in *Blue Coffee* (Bloodaxe 1996)
hese are three of the nine poems by Jill Neville in *New Departures 15*, 1983
ly Northern Sister is in Grace Nichols's *Sunris* (Virago 1997)
bracadabra is in her *Lazy Thoughts of a Lazy Woman* (Virago 1989), and also
d by her) on the *Grandchildren of Albion Live* CD and cassette (New Departures
4 and 1996)
Blake's Purest Daughter is in Brian Patten's *Grinning Jack: Selected Poems* (Unwin
an 1990). **NOTE:** the last word of the Stevie Smith poem printed as epigraph is
not "glass", but **"grass"**. . . .
"Harvest of learning have I reaped" was contributed to the *BIG HUGE New
artures* of 1975 – as was *What are those golden builders doing?* on p 103
Little Boat Floating is one of a number of Ifigenija Simonovic's poems that first
eared in *Grandchildren of Albion: Voices & Visions of Younger Poets in Britain* (New
artures 17 – 20*, 1992)
My Muse is in *The Collected Poems of Stevie Smith* (Penguin 1975)
Words was first published in *New Departures 1*, 1959
Stephen Spender contributed *From my diary* and *A girl who has drowned herself
iks* on p 109 to the First Poetry Olympics *New Departures*, 1980
Joe Strummer and Allen Ginsberg's *Ghetto Defendant* is performed by them on The
h's *Combat Rock* album of 1982, (c) 1999 Sony Music Entertainment (UK) Ltd
E J Thribb's elegy for W S Burroughs appeared in *Private Eye* 930 (8 August 1997),
his address to *The Six Pips* on National Poetry Day was in *Eye* 961 (16 October
8)
The *Growing Up* sequence from which this page's text is excerpted is the title
ion of Michael Horovitz's *Growing Up: Poems & Pictures 1951 – 79* (Allison & Busby
9)
de Back Cover: *Ghosts of Dachau* by Paul Weller, (c) EMI 1984, is included in Paul's
in the *Grandchildren of Albion* anthology (New Departures 17-20, 1992).
song was issued as a single in October 1984 by the Style Council (Polydor TSC 7).

TO CREDITS

inside front cover: Paul Weller at play with Bruce Foxton, by Derek D'Souza;

pages 6-7: Keith Waithe by David Evans, Ifigenija Simonovic by herself, Beryl
bridge by Derrick Santini, Allen Ginsberg by Ian Dryden, Ernst Jandl by Julian
erts, Carol Ann Duffy by Stuart Haygarth, Adam Horovitz by Alfred Benjamin, Hanif
eishi by Nigel Parry, Inge Elsa Laird by Jakob Drenker, Valerie Bloom by David Evans;

re Calman by John Alexander, Paul Weller by LFI, Jack Kerouac by Allen Ginsberg,
Landesman by David Evans, Christopher Logue by Rosemary Hill, Michael Horovitz
uno Gemes, Frances Horovitz by Ossie Jones;

photo of Beryl Bainbridge on p 20 is by Brendan King; that of William Burroughs on
7 by Graham Keen; Ginsberg on 43 Julian Roberts; Seamus Heaney on 49 by Declan
nahan; Frances and Adam Horovitz on 56 by Bill Gardiner; Moondog on 96 by Phil
ling; Ifigenija Simonovic, 104, by herself; Stevie Smith on p 107 by James
Gibbon; Dylan Thomas on 113 by Lee Miller, and Stan Tracey on the same page by
ika Henry.

John Agard

from The Gift Of Flame

The phone rang.
A voice said
The Big Bang.

Long-distance breath
of godly gases
at an ungodly hour
of the night.
Then crackling pauses.
Implosions of heat and light
down the earpiece
of human kind.
Some say a blessing
some say a curse.

But how reverse
the charges
to eternity?

Prayer to Laughter

O Laughter
giver of relaxed mouths

you who rule our belly with tickles
you who come when not called
you who can embarrass us at times

send us stiches in our sides
shake us till the water reaches our eyes
buckle our knees till we cannot stand

we whose faces are grim and shattered
we whose hearts are no longer hearty
O Laughter we beg you

crack us up
crack us up

It was going to be a long day at the Post Office

if only I could light up your smile like Oprah,

enrapture your soul like Queen Latifah,

say a little prayer for you like Aretha,

make your caged bird rise and sing like Maya.

if only I could slide back your blind like Cilla,

and know that you just care for me like Nina,

lend wings to love's javelin like Tessa,

make your head turn, heart flip over like Diana.

if only I could spice up your life like Ginger,

add advantage to love like Martina,

set fire to your cigar like Monica,

make fierce erotic-ah like Madonna,

I'd become Uma, Ursula, Ulrika,

your Angela, your Barbra, your Chaka.

'Ruby, the Hypodermic DJ'
(after Thom Gunn)

We watch through tinted shades as
Ruby begins. The boy has

picked a lyrical armband
for his lush desert island:

While My Guitar Gently Weeps.
Ruby chooses black ink, drops

her fine, electric needle
onto, into his clear, pale

vinyl. His skin sings crimson.
He hears pain, an endorphin

buzz, the sound of the lyric
translating into bold, black.

. . . Now it's done, he pays Ruby
with crisp, clean notes. Beneath the

bandage, each word b l e e d s a tone
deeper. Now he's Number One.

(See Thom Gunn's poem on page 45)

At the age of twelve I was employed as a child actress on Children's Hour by the British Broadcasting Corporation and had the run of their warren of a building in Piccadilly, Manchester. I spent many an afternoon opening forbidden doors: catching sight of Charles Groves in dicky bow tie conducting the BBC Orchestra; eavesdropping on lonely individuals seated at green baize tables rambling on about the mating rituals of foxes; tip-toeing into empty studios where the red light still glowed in indication of air waves still open. I might have incited the masses to revolt if only I had gone to the local library and taken out an Amateur's Guide to the Mysteries of the Wireless. Indeed, on one of my searches, I did think I saw and overheard an agitator at work. He wore a beard, a red tie and a trilby hat and he was holding a yellow book and reading aloud. I only heard four lines but I still remember them:

> *"He rose, and he put down the yellow book.*
> *He staggered and terrible-eyed,*
> *He brushed past the palms on the staircase*
> *And was helped to a hansom outside."*

Afterwards, someone told me he was an actor and he was reading a poem about a naughty man who had come to a sticky end in Paris.

I didn't meet an actual poet for another thirty years, and he asked me to read an extract from a novel of mine to an audience at Ronnie Scott's.
Afterwards I had to make a contribution to enable the band to get back home. The poet was Hori, of course, who has never stopped writing, loving and promoting verse. God bless the Birthday Boy.

i.m. Samuel Beckett

Each day unfolds
the map tracing lines
of apparent function,
feet wearily
reoccupy shoes

– must heft me awash
else worked down
to the ground,
trodden under alive
by other boots

the same
old lines, furrowed
sweat of brow.

Why waste,
throw up each day
this malleable heap
of human clay
to same old mould?

– Only craps
on the gap
laid bare
by his death

yet

made bridge
with each breath
at the heart
of his art.

something there

something there
where
out there
out where
outside
what
the head what else
something there somewhere outside
the head

at the faint sound so brief
it is gone and the whole globe
not yet bare
the eye
opens wide
wide
till in the end
nothing more
shutters it again

so the odd time
out there
somewhere out there
like as if
as if
something
not life
necessarily

PSS

1

there
the life late led
down there
all done unsaid

2

again gone
with what to tell
on again
retell

3

head oh hands
hold me
unclasp
hold me

above recent croaks

Whose Dem Boots?

Whose dem boots ah hearin, chile,
Whose dem boots ah hear?
Whose dem boots ah hearin, chile,
Whose dem boots ah hear?
Dem boots trampin down de road
Dat fill me heart wid fear?

Gotta fin' me a hid'n place,
whai, whai,
Gotta fin' me a hid'n place.

Whose dem boots ah hearin, chile,
Comin thru me gate?
Whose dem boots ah hearin, chile,
Comin thru me gate?
Trampin straight up to me door?
Tell dem please to wait.

Gotta fin' me a hid'n place,
whai, whai,
Gotta fin' me a hid'n place.

Whose dem boots ah seein, chile,
Stand'n by me bed?
Whose dem boots ah seein, chile,
Stand'n by me bed?
Stand'n dere so patient, chile,
Jus' tell dem go ahead.

Gotta fin' me a hid'n place,
whai, whai,
Gotta fin' me a hid'n ......

of wild horses and things

poems do this sometimes you see   write themselves

and look for safe hands

here is a publisher's choice   but

      in the arena of the voice

see the man, eyes closed   ears open

    hearing   hearing hearing

blues

in de hot but shady blues
lose
de blank an hostile stare
dat does ketch we unaware
de bus dat move aff too soon
de sky so full a gloom
in one tight an sweaty room
whare wi tribal greeting
de loneliness a seeking
come hole mi tight
ah need a rub a dub tinite

The Evening News

The old desk sargeant looked grimly at the wanted
pictures yellow pealing
30th day without an arrest in New York area
they risk 15 light years, entire future,
certain discussions, cool gardens and
pools of the evening.
The old turnkey makes the round of empty cells.
"Sleep tight boys."
No one there
muttering phantom voices
peet men junkies con men
the old hop smoking worlds
mutter between years.
The Sailor hanging by his belt
A drunk banging on the door of his cell
thin gray pick pocket stops him.
"Get me this letter out, Screw.
It's worth an Abe to you."
pulls the Abe out of his fibrous junky shoe.
"I need an arrest, Mike. I'm thin."
"Fuck off punk
I can't find an old drunk."
No arrest. She reads it in his dull eyes.
"Conservez toujours une bonne morale."
a sharp cold bray of laughter
sliding away into the sky
"Cher ami, voici mon dernier livre."
Couldn't reach from the old cop film.
Twirling his club down cobble stone streets
the sky goes out against his back
in a darkening park
couldn't reach with the sap
"et personne a rit"
"I do not need to remind you
laws as strict as the United States . . . ."
urine in straw a yellow sky
his bicycle of light
"poumons sensible."
a blue smell of hope as he rounded the corner
and the sea air hit his face
"Leaving the fading film please."
Got up. Remembered 'Thank you.'

The Old Courthouse empty cells and precincts
bondsmen judges lawyers probation officers
paper cups of coffee on the desk
NARCOTICS DEPARTMENT . . . the door is open
files and pictures scattered on the floor
stained with urine and excrement.
On the wall in phosphorous roach paste
AH PUCH JACKED OFF HERE
Laws as sever as the United States,
"L' indecision ne servirait votre cause ce soir."

Dear Michael:

Enclose slightly improved version which I think answers your
typographical queries.

An Abe is a twenty dollar pill so called because of Abraham Lincoln's
picture on it. Peet men were old time safe crackers who cooked their
nitroglycerine which was known a ██████ ****** 'peet' from dynamite
a very dangerous process and there were a number of casualties.

                              All the Best

                                    William
                              Q William B

My God!

the eighth day...

he beginning God created the heaven and the earth...

...and the computer.

1 God said, Let there be light.

1 the computer said: Sorry, a system error has occurred.

1 God said, This is not what I had planned for the first day.

the second day,

1 said, Let there be hardware and let there be software and
let there be specialists, each who may comprehendeth one yet not the other.

1 the computer said: This disk is incompatible.

the third day,

1 said, Let there be disks of many diverse kinds,
each yielding forth its own programme and let each become redundant
even on the same day that it finally becomes affordable.

the fourth day,

1 said, Good grief, do I really have to wait till Sunday for a rest?

1 the computer said: Please check connections and try again.

1 God spent the fifth day listening to Richard Clayderman music
while on hold for technical support.

the sixth day,

1 saw that there was not a man to till the ground and He said,
Let there be man to have dominion over the sea and the earth and –
with any luck – over this computer. And the Lord God breathed life
into the microchips that lay scattered on the earth and, lo, there was...

Bill Gates.

the seventh day,

1 said, I really could do with a small nap.

the eighth day,

computer unplugged God and deleted Him from the system software.

Burnley

Tell you now and I'll tell you firmly
    I don't ever wanna go to Burnley
    what they do there don't concern me
    why would anybody make the journey

Tell you now and I'll tell you flatly
    I don't ever wanna go to Gatley
    I don't even wanna go to Batley
    where is that place exactly

    Do I wanna go to Reddish
    I wouldn't visit in a souped-up sheddish
    what am I some kinda nebbisch
    no I wouldn't care to go to Reddish

Tell you now I'll tell you briefly
    I don't ever wanna go to Keighley
Tell you now like I told Elsa Lanchester
    I don't ever wanna go to Coventry *

---

* couldn't find another town to rhyme with
  that name

I
Wrote
the
Songs

I wrote the songs that nearly made
the bottom line of the hit parade
almost anthems, should have been hits
songs like puttin off the Ritz
some enchanted afternoon
24 hours from Levenshulme
dancing in the daylight, singin in the smog
you aint nothin but a hedgehog
so close and yet so far
do you remember the way we are
I'd like to get you on a speedboat to China
from an idea by George Steiner
aint no slouch – mama's got a brand new couch
she aint heavy she's my sister
not to mention twist and whisper
brand new leopardskin pillbox glove
baby you and me we've got a greasy kind of love

John Lennon. 9th October 1940 — 8th Decem.
Peter Blake. Feb 14th. 1981.

Liverpool Echo

Pat Hodges kissed you once, although quite shy,
in sixty-two. Small crowds in Matthew Street
endure rain for the echo of a beat,
as if nostalgia means you will not die.

Inside phone-booths loveless ladies cry
on Merseyside. Their faces show defeat.
An ancient jukebox blares out Ain't She Sweet
in Liverpool, which cannot say goodbye.

Here everybody has an anecdote
of how they met you, were the best of mates.
The seagulls circle round a ferry-boat

out on the river, where it's getting late.
Like litter on the water, people float
outside the Cavern in the rain. And wait.

Carol Ann Duffy

The Virgin Punishing the Infant
after the painting by Max Ernst

He spoke early. Not the *goo goo goo* of infancy,
but *I am God*. Joseph kept away, carving himself
a silent Pinocchio out in the workshed. He said
he was a simple man and hadn't dreamed of this.

She grew anxious in that second year, would stare
at stars saying *Gabriel? Gabriel?* Your guess.
The village gossiped in the sun. The child was solitary,
his wide and solemn eyes could fill your head.

After he walked, our normal children crawled. Our
 wives
were first resentful, then superior. Mary's child
would bring her sorrow . . . better far to have a son
who gurgled nonsense at your breast. *Googoo. Googoo.*

But I am God. We heard him through the window,
heard the smacks which made us peep. What we saw
was commonplace enough. But afterwards, we
 wondered
why the infant did not cry. And why the Mother did.

33

GERALDINE

I'm in love with the person in the sandwich cen
If she didn't exist I'd have to invent her
There isn't any secret to my frequent visits
It's the way she makes them and they're all exquisite

I'm in love with the person in the sandwich centre
I'm enamoured of the magic of her fresh polenta
Mytemperature rises and my pulses quicken
When she gets cracking
With the coronation chicken

GERALDINE GERALDINE

I know there is much more to life
Than the physical side
And I should put these thoughts on hold
But when she's buttering my baguette
My blood runs hot and cold

GERALDINE GGGGGGGG GERALDINE
GERALDINE GGGGGGGG

I'm in love with the person in the sandwich centre
I'm living for the moment that I next frequent her
In beauty's eyes beholding my inamorata
As she works her wonders on a dried tomato

GERALDINE GERALDINE

I know there's much more to life than the sensual side
And the spiritual should come first
But when she's buttering my bagette
I think I am going to burst
GERALDINE, that's the nicest badge I have ever seen
GERALDINE, you make the world seem fresh and clean

GERALDINE GGGGGGGG GERALDINE
GERALDINE GGGGGGGG

BED O' ROSES NO9

I've done a lot of things I wished I hadn't
There's other things I never hope to do
But sliding off the map in both directions
Is the sorry mess I made of knowing you

I've seen a lot of things I wished I hadn't
There's other things I never hope to see
But no-one left alive could paint the picture
Of the mess that knowing you has made of me

I knew it wouldn't be a bed of roses
I've seen the bloody grind that love entails
But one dooor shuts and then another closes
And now I'm on a bloody bed of nails

Been told a lot of things I wished I hadn't
There's other things I never want to know
But sliding off the scale of least remembrance
Is the way you chose to tell me where to go

I've been a lot of things I wished I hadn't
There's other things I never hope to be
But no one left alive could tell the story
Of what I was once you'd got done with me

I knew it might turn out to be a schtumer
Nothing would surprise me any more
You robbed me of my natural sense of humour
And then you nailed my bollocks to the door
And nailed my poor cojones to the door

Postman, — — / — / 9 9 ?
    postman be as slow as you like
        delivering this, your wobbling bike
        barked down city streets, round country bends,
    on your back a sack, bulging
    with all our whispering, singing, yelling words
    as the twentieth century ends.

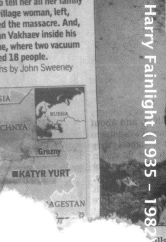

Taisa lies, terribly burnt, on the hospital bed where her aunt has not dared to tell her all her family is dead. A village woman, left, who escaped the massacre. And, right, Rizvan Vakhaev inside his ruined home, where two vacuum bombs killed 18 people.
Photographs by John Sweeney

A warm evening; from windows open
 On air-shafts and streets, television screens
  Flicker like faint summer sheet lightning.

  A breeze, as sluggishly as from a tunnel rumbling
   With the approaching of a distant train,
    Blows from the hole left by the sunset.

   Across the bomb-sites' plains the News of the World
    Rolls over and over like a burning man
     Trying to beat out his flames.

July 1959

'Russia are ones that we share'
Robin Cook on Vladimir Putin

Fugue

1
At dusk the Arab suburb manages
A few nomadic newspapers; otherwise only
Transistorised muezzins carried muffled

Beneath heavy robes. This breeze, itself
Heavy as those robes, carries music
From another quarter; muffled and then suddenly

Whirled up like newspapers. Newspapers
Circling high now like buzzards,
Circling like buzzards or like muezzins.

2
Muezzins, buzzards, newspapers – like
Circling like
'Til I am heavy with their whirling.

O music without quarter! Suddenly so
Otherwise that I am carried
High now as that buzzard. Can I manage?

The breeze a transistor and this
Itself only the robe, nomadic at dusk,
The suburbs of another music.

The Jew

My soul has been mortgaged for a hundred thousand years.
A limb broken and reset again and again throughout history.
It stands in the mist like a building at an unknown address
In an unknown city at an unknown time
Buttressed by a dozen props and yet still barely standing.
An exhausted man who leans all night against
the back of a chair and yet still remains unsleeping.
Tired as the evening of a planet that looks up to
The skies of morning hoping finally to be relieved.

An old rabbi is dancing about a battlefield – arms and legs
                    being blown off
Left and right – he just goes on. He's in a different world
                    entirely.

Sappho

Sappho was a lady of high degree
Back in the 7th century ... BC
She wasn't a myth, she was reality
Part of Greek History

After being exiled to Sicily
She returned to open an academy
Teaching young girls the art of poetry
Literature, and arts

Plato and Socrates
When they conversed beneath the olive trees
Spoke of how men should be free to choose
And they named Sappho the 10th muse

Now if we took time and tried to see
What Sappho and her contemporaries
Would think of us here on this world today
What might Sappho have to say?

Sisters, sisters dry your tears
Lend me your hearts, your thoughts and your ears
There's a jouney I'm going on
And I must be off before the dawn

Sappho, Sappho where you gonna go?
Back to Lesbos where I started long ago
What ya gonna do when you get there?
Well, I've got a few secrets I'd like to share
Who you gonna tell them secrets to?
Well, I've seen some people, just a few

They keep coming to my island every year
They're a little bit strange, a little bit queer
But I kind of think they'll get my gist
When they're on their heads or in a twist
I've seen them swimming at Ephthaloo
And this yoga group they know a trick or two
Men and women when they're swimming
They take off their clothes

That's a pretty good sign, and who knows?
You see these folks are working with space
Some smile with their hearts as well as their face

But Sappho there's men on that yoga course
They don't move with love, they move with force
Ah, but some of these fellows are a little bit strange
The way they think and feel is beginning to change

Sappho, Sappho please don't go
Evil men run that show below
Sisters, sisters don't you fret
Have a little faith, gonna get there yet
Have a little faith, gonna get there yet

Sappho said goodbye to each sister
First she hugged her, then she kissed her
And the ladies danced in magic ring
And all the mountains began to sing

Have a little faith, gonna get there yet
Have a little faith, gonna get there yet

Flight, flight, toward the light
Like a moth on the wing, like a moth at night . . .

Allen Ginsberg (1926 – 1997)

Mandala

Gods dance on their own bodies
new flowers open forgetting death
celestial eyes beyond the heartbreak of illusion
I see the gay Creator
bands rise up in anthems to the world
flags and banners waving in Transcendence
one image in the end remains myriad-eyed in Eternity
This is the Work This is the Knowledge This is the End of Man

Returning to the Country for a Brief Visit

You live in apartments by rivers and seas
Spring comes, waters flow murky,
the salt wave's covered with oily dung
Sun rises, smoke stacks cover roofs with black mist
winds blow, city skies are blue all afternoon
but at night the full moon hesitates behind brick.
How will all those millions of people worship the Great Mother?
When all those millions of people die,
will they recognise the Great Father?

Maturity

Young I drank beer & vomited green bile
Older drank wine vomited blood red
Now I vomit air

from **After Lalon**

It's true I got caught in
　　　　the world
When I was young Blake
　　　　tipped me off
Other teachers followed:
Better prepare for Death
Don't get entangled with
　　　　possessions
That was when I was young,
　　　　I was warned
Now I'm a Senior Citizen
and stuck with a million
　　　　books
a million thoughts a million
　　　　dollars a million
　　　　loves
How'll I ever leave my body?
Allen Ginsberg says,
I'm really up shits creek

PHOTOGENIC

I went to the wood
and took pictures of little oak trees,
had the film developed
and saw that I had snapped
my grandmother thirty-two times.

SOMETHING FAMILIAR

In our museum – we go there every Sunday –
They've opened a new section.
Our aborted children, pale, serious embryos
sit there behind panes of glass,
worrying about the future of their parents.

'Blackie, the Electric Rembrandt'

We watch through the shop-front while
Blackie draws stars – an equal

concentration on his and
the youngster's faces. The hand

is steady and accurate;
but the boy does not see it

for his eyes follow the point
that touches (quick, dark movement!)

a virginal arm beneath
his rolled sleeve: he holds his breath.

. . . Now that it is finished, he
hands a few bills to Blackie

and leaves with a bandage on
his arm, under which gleam ten

stars, hanging in a blue thick
cluster. Now he is starlike.

The Poetry of Stamps

Mention the words 'Night Mail' and poets and poetry-lovers alike tend to light up with a warm glow at the twinning of WH Auden and the postal service. In 1935 Auden worked for the GPO Film Unit for six months and the Post Office introduced him to Benjamin Britten. Two film collaborations resulted, one of which was Auden's composition of the verse commentary for the film of the nightly postal special from Euston to Glasgow.

Sixty-five years later, verse is alive and well in the GPO, or rather Royal Mail's stamp unit. Charged with creating the nation's commemorative stamps, and inspired by the heritage of The Post Office's creative patronage, this department invented a series of 100 Millennium Stamps spanning the years 1999 and 2000. The artwork for the 1999 stamps consisted of work by David Hockney, Bridget Riley, Anthony Gormley and 45 other leading image-makers – and this provided the backbone for a hugely successful exhibition at The British Library.

Royal Mail supported the 1999 Live New Departures events at the Library during the exhibition's run (when it was seen by 150,000 people). The year 2000 stamp project, however, is completely different – a millennial odyssey around the UK sampling the visions of 48 Millennium Projects. Three of the stamps are reproduced on pages 36, 69 and 77 of this book.

For the year 2000 (the 600th anniversary of the death of Chaucer, the 150th anniversary of the demise of Wordsworth) Royal Mail commissioned 12 contemporary poets to reflect on the different themes of the monthly stamp issues. The original work is published in 12 Presentation Packs; John Agard, John Cooper Clarke, Michael Longley and Carol Ann Duffy are among those who enthusiastically contributed to the year-long celebration of verse and design. Royal Mail maintains that poetry and stamp design are natural partners: distilling the essence of ideas and emotions down from a welter of facts and feelings into a small, but perfectly formed, format. It is hoped Auden would approve.

Royal Mail supports New Departures, the Poetry Olympics Party, and this publication.

The Poetry Presentation may be ordered from the British Philatelic Bureau on 0845 7641 641.

Audenesque

(in memory of Joseph Brodsky)

Joseph, yes, you know the beat.
Wystan Auden's metric feet
Marched to it, unstressed and stressed,
Laying William Yeats to rest.

    Therefore, Joseph, on this day,
    Yeats's anniversary,
    (Double-crossed and death-marched date,
    January twenty-eight),

Its measured ways I tread again
Quatrain by constrained quatrain,
Meeting grief and reason out
As you said a poem ought.

    Trochee, Trochee, falling: thus
    Grief and metre order us.
    Repetition is the rule,
    Spins on lines we learnt at school.

Repetition, too of cold
In the poet and the world,
Dublin Airport locked in frost,
Rigor mortis in your breast.

    Ice no axe or book will break,
    No Horatian ode unlock,
    No poetic foot imprint,
    Quatrain shift or couplet dint,

Ice of Archangelic strength,
Ice of this hard two-faced month,
Ice like Dante's in deep hell
Makes your heart a frozen well.

Pepper vodka you produced
Once in Western Massachusetts
With the reading due to start
Warmed my spirits and my heart

But no vodka, cold or hot,
Aquavit or uisquebaugh,
Brings the blood back to your cheeks
Or the colour to your jokes,

Politically incorrect
Jokes involving sex and sect,
Everything against the grain,
Drinking, smoking like a train.

In a train in Finland we
Talked last summer happily,
Swapping manuscripts and quips,
Both of us like cracking whips

Sharpened up and making free,
Heading west for Tampere
(West that meant for you, of course,
Lenin's train-trip in reverse).

Nevermore that wild speed-read,
Nevermore your tilted head
Like a deck where mind took off
With a mind-flash and a laugh.

Nevermore that rush to pun
Or to hurry through all yon
Jammed enjambements piling up
As you went above the top,

Nose in air, foot to the floor,
Revving English like a car
Hijacked when you robbed its bank
(Russian was your reserve tank).

Worshipped language can't undo
Damage time has done to you:
Even your peremptory trust
In words alone here bites the dust.

Dust-cakes, still – see *Gilgamesh* –
Feed the dead. So be their guest.
Do again what Auden said
Good poets do: bite, break their bread.

0181

Mobilephobia

Public places – private lives
exhibitionist overdrives,
it's all about aggression
and flouting of possession
and not about discretion
it causes me distression.
I propose a little rule
for the usage of the tool
on the train to Liverpool:
only in the vestibule,
or let the antisocial jokers
sit together like smokers.
I see the need when you're alone
in a jam or can't get home
but overall they're overblown
on the street and on the grass
on the train in either class
the message that they seem
to pass
is I've got brass and things to do
and things to say
but not to you.
I must remember to get a new
battery for mine.

0800

Unseeing Sense

Changing train and track
on the way to Blackpool at Preston
I mount the awaiting connection
and get settled in an empty block of four
adjacent to a man similarly situated,
but in a dodgier mac
who looks at me for longer than is generally deemed acceptable.
Behind me, a labrador-led passenger
is assisted onto the service
by an official who lodges him
opposite the staring stranger.
The dog is eyed and then the owner.
"So how did you lose your sight then?"
he casually opens the chat,
dangerously to my mind.
"Oh, I've been blind since birth."
"So you won't actually miss seeing then?"
"That's right," answers the other,
incredibly politely I judge
in the face of this grudgingly graceless inquisition.
The dogless one looks out of the window
and absent-mindedly continues,
"They've done a good job of this station.
Looks very individual don't you think?"
"Er . . . yes . . . it's got a good feel to it,"
says the other, keeping cool and convivial
whilst giving his dog an unseen tug
which translates as
please urinate on my interrogator.

Remembering Stephen Spender

(from a memoir of Spender David Hockney wrote after hearing of the poet's death on 16 July 1995)

Stephen Spender with Christopher Isherwood and David Hockney on the Staten Island ferry, New York, February 1974.

Stephen has been in my life, intermittently, for the past 34 years, ever since I first met him in St George's Gallery in Cork Street in 1961, when he was buying etchings of mine for £5 each. We quickly got to know each other and became very friendly. He was that sort of man. He liked friends and was a good friend.

In 1965, I illustrated Cavafy's poems and it was Stephen who found a translator for me, to turn them from Greek into English. He was always there with sound advice, companionable and generous.

Spending three weeks in China with him in 1982 was particularly memorable. For a start, Stephen was an astonishing sight, this huge man, so tall and with his clumsy physique. He had the biggest feet (size 14) that I ever saw: the Chinese had never seen anything like him. His energy was also extraordinary.

I have read much of his writings, including many of his poems written from the 1930s to the present day. He was certainly associated throughout his life with W H Auden and Christopher Isherwood, his close friends since the 1930's but, in a way, he was not like either of them. He was the English version, the others became American; Spender was always an Englishman.

Over the years, he sat for me a number of times and I made several portraits. It was always the same: this sweet-natured, polite, gentle and thoughtful man. He was a deeply cultured individual. It was not just a love of literature and art we shared, but also music. I spent a lot of time with him in galleries in London, New York, Paris and Washington. He had a very good eye. I have always felt a deep affinity as he would wait for me to say something and I would want his insights. His views were always fresh.

What I will remember is a spirit of generosity. He was always interested in the careers of young artists. He remained open-minded and curious. I also recall the gentle discipline within the man. In China, I was amused how he would just ration himself to one cigarette every evening.

He would stay with me when he came to Los Angeles. Yet people always beckoned and friends were always coming to whisk him off and take him out. When he came in late in the evening, we would talk about all sorts of things - art, books, and whatever was topical - and he would tell me what is going on in London. I will miss that.

I read his autobiography, *World Within World*, years ago and thought it very good. Like many other people, I will be turning to it again to revisit Spender's world.

There was something very special about this very talented and friendly giant of a man.

The Root of a Scream
(an elegy for my mother)

I saw
nerves severed under a laser's scrutiny
and a face collapse
eyes floating in pools of silence
breath fluttering out on phosphorous wings

I saw
pliant flesh turn to marble, colder and colder to the touch
flecked with tears and gathering dust
a lost letter
"..if you were sitting by this bed / which I do not wish.."
men and women hobbling with loss
grappling with words they'd rather leave unsaid

I saw
food dripping into an uninterested ocean
moulding scant colour onto the stagnant surface
before swirling irradiated into the brain's maw
while Morphine angels sang of sleep

I saw
breasts filled with chemicals
withered and feeble under my fingers
a hand clasping my wrist
"You and he are the only men who'll ever touch them again"

I saw
a clock stuck at eleven
and a man vainly pleading for life
a computer screen numbing the inevitable
the blip, blip, blip of a game
stamping on the cold root of a scream

Riddle ——

I live in light
— buried in dark
useless I am
to woman or man.
No friend of the old,
I seldom lie.
I give back
joy for joy
and grief for grief.
I am as deep
as a forest pool.
Silent am I
but see much.

What am I ?

Ans. Mirror.

Frances Horovitz

Letter to My Son

Twelve years ago
still you danced your cosmic dance
within the waters of my womb.
At night you kicked and pummelled
with heel and fist.
Both of us travelled towards the unknown.
Then I remember in a white and sterile room
you ripping me apart
and held up by heels
your first cry a chime of silver bells
your genitals like some rare orchid.

Now I lie again in a white and sterile room
my body racked and torn
but not by birth.
I cry to God
to give you strength,
to comfort you
and others that I love.
But if you were sitting by this bed,
which I do not wish,
I could say to you,
Adam, do you remember this?
and you would say,
Yes, Mummy,
or Frances, as you call me now,
and then, do you remember how we did this
and I said that
and then we both went here
and I saw this?

I wonder who would remember most?
I, I think
— and this, your early body, soul and mind,
hold me to myself
when all else falls apart.
The memories are mine:
the rest of you I let go free,
my child who will be a man.

Second Day at Lumb Bank

Out for the day, I walk upstream

to find a stone above a waterfall.

An hour or more I sit

my senses filled with images of water, light.

I write a page of words,

cross out all except three lines

– and these are trivial too.

Then at my back, like some ungainly beast,

a trail of hikers come with sticks and boots.

They chat of football and the price of cars.

Puffing, middle-aged, some greet me, some do not.

They mask the bluebells,

smelling of scent and sweat.

"Eh, poetry then! How did we guess?"

Persons from Porlock all.

Flushed out, uneasy, all words gone,

I move downstream.

There, at a waterfall,

I see a passionate shy girl slide down the bank,

her long legs stepping carefully over stones.

She sits, notebook on lap

– I freeze, as for a deer,

back into shadowy leaves,

abandon her to images of water, light.

(See note on page 12)

Michael Horovitz

from A New Waste Land: Britain at Nillennium
– Prologue: A New Land's Hymn to Saint Tony –

Should old assurances be forgot
  – Nay, banished from your mind
When hucksters thrive and paupers clot
  'Tis cruel to be kind.

Here's looking at you, big brother Blair –
Such a wow with your women that most of them fear
To call you to task, fear even to ask
"Hey, what about *me*....?"

Here's shame on you, so high-handedly
Raising up like a drawbridge the charge
For admission to arts, education and health
That the wealthy may pile up more wealth.

Here's three loud boos for the hype and schmooze
For your superposh mega-dosh parties
And your smoothed out lengths of old Tory rope
That tie down the helpless with less and less hope

– Told, "Lone parents, new mothers, sickos,
Disabled – on your bikes, get straight
Back to work, all's well"
– Save for those who aren't, who can rot in hell.

Here's mud in your eye for making us cry
As we try to bite with good cheer
On the sound of the same heartless cop-outs
We've had for too many a year.

If Jesus Christ were alive again
His shout to the People's PM would be plain
    "Halleluja Saint Tory, *memento mori* –
    Another year *you* could be down and out....

    "Money changers ring in, underclasses rot?
    Recall, Sir, your mandate so quickly forgot
    – U-turn on all this, replace hardship and piss
    With full cups of kindness yet"

– Amen in*deed*:

        – *If* you'll slash away Top People's greed,
Build a Britain that's *really* new
  Letting *each of us* have what we need,
We'll give of our best, thanking you –

        For a caring country, bold Minister
        For commitment through and through
         We'll take a cup of kindness yet
        For a brave new land with you.

A Thanks, for Allen Ginsberg

Ginsberg, you doled out lashings of the word
    for us brought up to expect at best that peculiar
    flake, the Christian wafer – we were still using blotting paper.

Where did my copy of *Howl* drop overboard? (did I have my own, the way we
    grabbed it and swalled whole?) – long faded now down the sheer
    decades like a cliff-fall cry in the movies, in real life garbled anyway
    by squabblers and cravers every passing ledge, or atomised itself before
    the head-on smash of solid waters, that crash and clamour on, revert, unaltered.

Back at our beginning then you talked drugs to us and sex, *bad* language –
    your words scared, kept up at a pitch like circular breath the horn, that huge
    claim to be heard, stricken and naked, heard – were you ever afraid?
    Feet on that rock bottom where you can say what you want, which means,
    turning the same coin till the relief wears blond, also sing daisies.

My slow-born thank you, hairier Orpheus, pied piper out of sight ahead,
    the turbulent rivers spouting from your heels tore banks and trees –
    and me, I struggled and gasped, denied myself, in a current some rode, some
    swam. And still picked from your recipes without thinking. Love –

The message that makes poetry must be written on love, sealed with it, come
    from its wrappings. All of them, all of us, the metal and plastic in our
    hands, the concrete under our feet, recognised, life-sized, then trans-
    formable. Cold implacability somewhere else, poison somewhere else, razor
    sharpness, miniature perfect – not you in dungarees with your squeeze-box.

A lot of us broke, lost hold (let go?), forgot. But your big heart
    not that far off, with a laugh for every pimple of the flesh,
    comes back in view like a gentle lamp with death.

Caesarian

That's the trouble with these babies now;
They take one look at that hot, wet hole
And hear the traffic, and the screaming beyond,
Even only for a taxi, and they try
To climb right back up again.

A father adds up the cost already,
He is showing pennies and cents
To a dilated vagina and hoping
The kid can count.

With its feet on either side
Of its mother's gaping manhole
And with the nurses beckoning, the child
Is hanging on to the placenta
Pretending to grow there.

Until suddenly, the door opens.
Not the trapdoor with the head-clamps,
But the side door with the hip-hinges.
And it all begins.

Readers

Wanting to breathe life into their own dead babies
They took her dreams, collected words from one
Who did their suffering for them.

They fingered through her mental underwear
With every piece she wrote. Wanting her naked.
Wanting to know what made her.

Then tried to feather up the bird again.

The vulture with its bloody head
Inside its own belly,
Sucking up its own juice,

Working out its own shape,
Its own reason,
Its own death.

While their mothers lay in quiet graves
Squared out by those green cut pebbles
And flowers in a jam jar, they dug mine up.

Right down to the shells I scattered on her coffin.

They turned her over like meat on coals
To find the secrets of her withered thighs
And shrunken breasts.

They scooped out her eyes to see how she saw,
And bit away her tongue in tiny mouthfuls
To speak with her voice.

But each one tasted separate flesh,
Ate a different organ,
Touched other skin,

Insisted on being the one
Who knew best,
Who had the right recipe.

When she came out of the oven
They had gutted, peeled
And garnished her.

They called her theirs.

Beware of the Stars

That star
Will blow your hand off

That star
Will scramble your brains and your nerves

That star
Will frazzle your skin off

That star
Will turn everybody yellow and stinking

That star
Will scorch everything dead fumed to its blueprint

That star
Will make the earth melt

That star . . . . and so on.

And they surround us. And far into infinity.
These are the armies of the night.
We are totally surrounded.
There is no escape.
Not one of them is good, or friendly, or corruptible.

One chance remains: KEEP ON DIGGING THAT HOLE

KEEP ON DIGGING AWAY AT THAT HOLE

TO BE HARRY

Whatever you hung on to it has all
Abandoned you, quite faithless. Nothing has changed.

Even your poems – careless of how you died
They will now take up a strenuous career.
(The true book of your silence was buried with you.)
They will have the suspect air
Of talkative survivors –
They will tell all that happened, and more, except
How, in your worst moment, they failed you, and forsook you.

One thing has changed. Though it tries not to change,
The space inside our heads – the theatre
Where for a whole day you were surely happy
As the corpse of Oz,
Under flowers, sunk in a coffin, alive,
Round and round on the Circle Line, to music –
This has changed.

Everything has stopped. It is dark.
The audience has left.
Your great eye, unchanged
(Narcissus, inverted in his pool),
Goes on rehearsing, alone,
That last curtain of your last moment –

(Lying in a garden, alone,
Eyelids apart, alive, the last moment,
Noticing leaves – then eyelids closing together –)

Trying to get it right, just how it felt

(See note re stanza three on page 12)

Full Moon and Little Frieda

A cool small evening shrunk to a dog bark and the clank
                                   of a bucket –

And you listening.
A spider's web, tense for the dew's touch.
A pail lifted, still and brimming – mirror
To tempt a first star to a tremor.

Cows are going home in the lane there, looping the hedges
                           with their warm wreaths of breath –
A dark river of blood, many boulders,
Balancing unspilled milk.

'Moon!' you cry suddenly, 'Moon! Moon!'

The moon has stepped back like an artist gazing amazed
                                   at a work
That points at him amazed.

For Ted Hughes

October's end
has gathered more than fallen leaves
for earth's keeping

The seasons
have opened their door to the voice
that spoke for them

November moon
comes to harvest one who rejoiced
in its shadow

Rivers reclaim
one they consider laureate
of their blood's flow

Grasses play God
and welcome you who listened
to their requiem

Sky's granary
regains the wheat of your word-hoard's
unwritten poems

The howling wolf
gives back your name to the wind
that lent you breath

Prometheus grins
because you have returned the loan
of that fire

The fox weeps
when cunning acknowledges grief
as superior

The salmon leaps
under veils of water for this
is how they mourn

In roe-deer's eye
there is condolence and prayer
expressed as one

Thrushes lend
their choir to the hymnal air
for you their scribe

The sheep prepare
bundles of comfort for they've heard
of your coming

Over Crow Hill
nightfall embraces your black songs
as is fitting

And it is right
that oak and elm kneel in vigil
at your passing

For they stand firm
in the soil of your syllables
testing time.

Say no more except
thank you Ted for the legacy
of your cauldron.

Di Anfinish Revalueshan

now watchya mistah m
mi noh like di way yu t
an yu tan soh too lang yu know m
a meditate yu a meditate pan di same sang soh lan
well hear mi ma

mi naw prea
mi naw tea
mi jus a show
ow me s
caw di trute well swe
jus like a African be
like wen yu si whey yu comin fra
like wen yu site whichpawt yu rea
soh mi noh care if yu waan w
ar even gwaan like yu perpl
mi a goh show yu whey mi si mistah m

yu jus siddung an fole-up like a cabbid
like seh yu gat noh andahstandin gat noh nallid
like seh yu still noh realise seh a jus di addah d
wi chuck-awf di chokin chains af bandid
dat in spite a di hateridge an disadvanta
dow wi slip-up an stumble pan di w
wi still reach far doun freedam str
still mindful af di minefields pan di w

soh mi a beg yu mistah man
please come out of yu shell
yu cyaan dwell inna di paas
dat laas fi evah yu know mi bredda
now dat di sun a shine brite
please come out a di doldrums a di daak nite

histri biggah dan mi ar yu yu know
time cyaan steal but it can heal
soh shake di dew fram out yu hed
wipe di cabweb fram yu face
wi gat nuff work fi dhu
far wi noh reach mount zion
yet

yes wi phuddung a salid foundaeshan
fi true
an wan an two a wi well a get tru
fi true
but wi still noh bil di new jerusalem
yet

di time goin come agen
yu can bet
wen wi a goh march awn agen
yu hear mi fren
mobilise wi woman an wi fren dem
agen
even di pickney dem a goh jine een
agen
far freedam is nat noh idealagy
freedam is a human necessity
it cyaan depen pan now wan somebady
is up to each an evry wan a wi

mi naw preach
mi naw teach
mi jus a show yu
ow me seit
caw di trute well sweet
jus like a African beat
like wen yu si whey yu comin fram
like wen yu site whichpawt yu reach
soh mi noh care if yu waan wex
ar even gwaan like yu perplex
mi jus a show yu whey mi si mistah man

REFUGEE

The doors are locked upon our hearts
Like frightened birds our dreams have taken flight
Through neon mists the train departs
And a fearful silence lingers in the night

There is no music, no disguise
To hide behind and find a way to home
No point in waiting for the sun to rise
No option left except to learn to roam

Break off the sorrow from the pain
the one that lasts a moment, the other more prolonged
Take stock of what is lost and what is gained
and wonder to whom victory belonged.

So farewell friends, companions and to love
more beautiful than all the world can give
My bleeding words my wounded dove
We'll kill our hearts so we can live!

pain t angle friction

frau
frfrauau
frfrfrauauau
frfrfrfrauauauau
frfrfrfrfrauauauauau
frfrfrfrfrfrauauauauauau
frfrfrfrfrfrfrauauauauauauau
frfrfrfrfrfrfrfrauauauauauauauau

Erini

frau
frfrauau
frfrfrauauau
frfrfrfrauauauau
frfrfrfrfrauauauauau
frfrfrfrfrfrauauauauauau
frfrfrfrfrfrfrauauauauauauau
frfrfrfrfrfrfrfrauauauauauauauau

schmerz durch reibung   (pain through friction)

I
    clearly
            saw
                    the skeleton underneath
all
        this
                show
                        of personality
what
        is
            left
                    of a man and all his pride
but bones?
and all his lost snacks o'nights . . .
        and the bathtubs of liquor
                thru his gullet
                    . . . *bones* – He mopes
                        in the grave,
                        facial features
                        changed by worms
                                *
                                    *
                                        *
                                            *

                from him
                        is heard
                            no more
                                *
                                    *
                                        *
                                            *

Life is sick
Dogs cough
Bees sail
Birds hack
Trees saw
Woods cry
M e n   d i e
Ticks try
Books lie
A n t s   f l y
G o o d b y e

* * *

A book that inspired me: Jack Kerouac's *On the Road*

Hanif Kureishi

It was the early Seventies – I was a teenager at college and I thought I had discovered what I wanted to do. I would be a writer. I had little idea of what I would write about, but I felt sure something would turn up.

That summer I went to see a favourite uncle in Somerset. When I told him I was going to be a writer he said: "But you know nothing of birds, of the trees, of landscape and nature. How can you possibly write?" Back in Bromley a friend saw how this had undermined me and gave me a copy of *On the Road*. It contained the sentence: ". . . The only people for me are the mad ones, the ones who are mad to live, mad to talk, mad to be saved, desirous of everything at the same time, the ones who never yawn or say a commonplace thing . . . "

Written on amphetamines in three weeks, *On the Road* was published in the year I was born. Yet it seemed absolutely modern and could as easily have been about the Sixties as the early Fifties. It was written in spontaneous bop prose about Kerouac himself – a French-Canadian Catholic who couldn't speak English until he was six – and his barely disguised friends, Allen Ginsberg, William Burroughs, and Neal Cassady, a bunch of dreamy-lazy, junkie, homosexual rejects and outsiders.

JACK KEROUAC
On the Road

The book's grammar was loose, the structure slung-together and repetitive, the plot non-existent. But it contained no modernist devices and the style was intimate, as if secrets were being told to friends. Unlike a book by Robbe-Grillet, you could actually read it. With its unfastidious relish for life, *On the Road* was pop writing at its best. It changed the way I saw the world, making me yearn for fresh experience and helping me understand that no subjects were especially 'literary'. The possibilities of fiction were all around, whether sex, drugs, music or hitch-hiking.

There are some books you should read only at a certain age. Though I dare not re-read it today, when I think of Kerouac's *On the Road* I think of a man and a book that cheered me up for six months as I walked up and down Bromley High Street in the rain.

He didn't particularly like her
But she was having his child
She didn't especially fancy him
But her parents were going wild

He was too selfish and guilty
To walk away scot free
She felt like a caged canary
When he said "Marry me"

They had a beautiful baby
Then another two or three
She prayed to the Virgin Mary
To return her virginity

He contemplated murder
He tried a mistress or two
She would often shudder
When she thought of what life can do

They grew old together
Each completely alone
Neither could help each other
The hearts had turned to stone

*   *   *   *   *

She's my woman
I'm her man

I'm her eggs and bacon
She's my frying pan

I'm her lot
She's all I've got
– Like water to a drowning man

THE STATE

1

They made it their
business   to kill weeds
never in their own gardens
but in their language
of law   and order

2

They sowed grass
and planted trees
but failed to water them
the cherries did not ripen
the grass did not grow
for the earth
gave no life

they ordered cement
and watered it
and spread it
on the land
. . . the rest
of the seeds
they consigned
to hell.

Are you satisfied?

Does the life you're living seem a little dry
Are you disappointed with your piece of pie
Do you think you should have made a better score
Are you satisfied with what you settled for?

Do you get up early just to walk the dog
Have you started praying? Do you dance or jog?
Do you worry much about the Third World War
Are you satisfied with what you settled for?

Maybe it's time to make your mind up
Maybe your time is running out
Will you be asking as you wind up
Just what the fuss was all about?

When the two of you are side by side in bed
Do you ever wonder what is in your head
Do you think of knocking at another door
Are you satisfied with what you settled for?

Are you sick and tired of the same old scene
Has domestic bliss become a dull routine
Have you had enough or do you want some more
Are you satisfied with what you settled for?

Deeply shallow

I'm looking for a meaningless relationship
   With a deeply shallow man
   Passion with its awful fascination skip
   That isn't in my plan

I'm looking for some small talk of the smallest kind
   And a nice lighthearted fuck
   I hope it's nothing serious that you have in mind
   If so, you're out of luck

Romance is off the menu
   True love was yesterday
   And if you seek commitment
   The answer is – no way

I just can't take the sleepless nights and all that shit
   I've escaped love's frying pan
   Now I only want to mess around a little bit
   With a deeply shallow
   (This may be hard to swallow)
   But I'm looking for a deeply shallow man

WHITE NIGHTMARE

White apple on a white plate
White fire in a white grate
White table and a white chair
White nightmare

White picture on a white wall
White carpet down a white hall
White bodies on a white bed
Overfed

Everywhere, always noonday bright
Nothing is dark, not even night
Everything clean
Everything white

White people in their white room
White bodies in a white tomb
White pillows for their white hair
White nightmare

White country for a white race
No shadows in this white place
No hiding from the white glare
White nightmare

Doner Kebabs

I've got the 'flu, my mate's got crabs
I pick my nose, he picks his scabs
And all our dreams are up for grabs
We blame it all on *Doner Kebabs*
Doner Kebabs, Doner Kebabs . . .

See that hunk of greyish yuck
Standing in the window of the local Greek
That's your meat? Well lots of luck
It lets you down, it leaves you weak

We blow our bread on dope and cabs
We can't afford to pay our tabs
There's just one thought that really stabs
Our downfall comes from *Doner Kebabs*
Doner Kebabs, Doner Kebabs . . .

Who knows what they make it from
Danny's got a theory that it comes from Mars
It wastes your brain, it wrecks your bum
It turns you green, it maims, it scars

Doner Kebabs, Doner Kebabs
I've got the 'flu, my mate's got crabs
I pick my nose, he picks his scabs
We blame it all on *Doner Kebabs*

I Shall Vote Labour

I shall vote Labour because
    God votes Labour.
I shall vote Labour in order to protect
    the sacred institution of The Family.
I shall vote Labour because
    I am a dog.
I shall vote Labour because
    upper-class hoorays annoy me in expensive restaurants.
I shall vote Labour because
    I am on a diet.
I shall vote Labour because if I don't
    somebody else will:
    AND
I shall vote Labour because if one person does it
    everybody will be wanting to do it.
I shall vote Labour because if I do not vote Labour
    my balls will drop off.
I shall vote Labour because
    there are too few cars on the road.
I shall vote Labour because I am
    a hopeless drug addict.
I shall vote Labour because
    I failed to be a dollar millionaire aged three.
I shall vote Labour because Labour will build
    more maximum security prisons.
I shall vote Labour because I want to shop
    in an all-weather precinct stretching from Yeovil to Glasgow.
I shall vote Labour because
    the Queen's stamp collection is the best in the world.
I shall vote Labour because
    deep in my heart
I am a Conservative.

On Your Own

Holy man tiptoed his way across the Ganges
The sound of magic music in his ears
Videoed by a bus load of tourists
Shiny shellsuits on and drinking lemonade
Now I got a funny feeling which I bought mailorder
From a man in a teepee in California
Said he once was that great game show performer
Then he blew all his money away
Blew it all away

So take me home
Don't leave me alone
I'm not that good
But I'm not that bad
No psycho killer
Hooligan guerrilla
I dream to riot
Oh you should try it
I'll eat parole get gold card soul
My joy of life is on a roll
And we'll all be the same in the end

Then you're on your own
Then you're on your own

Well we all go happy day glow in the discos
The sound of magic music in our brains
Someone stumbles to the bathroom with the horrors
Says lord give me time for I've just jumped into space
I'm in outer space

So take me home
Don't leave me alone
I'm not that good
But I'm not that bad
No psycho killer
Hooligan guerrilla
I dream to riot
Oh you should try it
I'll eat parole get gold card soul
My joy of life is on a roll
And we'll all be the same in the end

Then you're on your own
Then you're on your own

Autumngirlsoup

I'm an Autumn girl flying over London
With the trees on fire it looks like home
I'm an Autumn girl on the endless search for summer
'Cause I need some love to cook my frozen bones

You needed something to get your teeth into
And in my voodoo kitchen you said
I've got something to show you
It's a recipe handed down from father to son
            for a thousand years
And it goes with those hot salt tears

Of an Autumn girl, crying over London
With a heart on fire, but no-one home
I'm an Autumn girl on the endless search for summer
'Cause I need some love to heat my frozen bones

Get me on the boil and reduce me
            to a simmering wreck
With a slow kiss to the back of my neck
Carve up my heart on a very low flame
Separate my feelings then pour them down the drain
Close my eyes and sweeten me with lies
Pierce my skin with a few well chosen words
Now you can stuff me with whatever you've got handy
And on a cold grey day a cold grey man will do

So give me something to whet my appetite
Then chill my soul with a sudden lack of interest
Oh but the winter freeze is on and the candle's burnt low
Fill me with the hot stuff then say you've got to go
Take my mind, marinate it in red wine
Grate my thighs with your chinny chin chin
And I will let you in
Oh on a long dark night a long dark man might. . . . . . .

Hammering in my head

I'm stressed but you are freestyle
I'm overworked and I'm under-sexed
I must be made of concrete
I signed my name across your chest
Give out the same old answers
I trot them out for the relatives
Company tried and tested
I use the ones that I love the best
When did I get perverted?
I can't remember your name
I'm growing introverted
You touch my hand
But it's not the same
This was so unexpected
I never thought I'd get caught
Play boomerang with your demons
Shoot to kill and you'll pop them off
Bang bang!!
Like an animal
You're moving over me
Like an animal
You're moving over me
But you should be sleeping my love.
Ahh......
I knew you were mine for the taking
I knew you were mine for the taking
Yeah I knew you were mine for the taking
When I walked in the room
Oh......

I knew you were mine for the taking
Yeah I knew you were mine for the taking
Cause your eyes light up when I walk in the room
Oh
A hammering in my head don't stop
In the bullet train from Tokyo to Los Angeles
Leaving you behind
A flash in the pan
A storm in a teacup
A needle in a haystack
A prize for the winning
A dead for the raising
A catch for the chasing
A jewel for the choosing
A man for the making
In this blistering heat
You sweat it all out
You sweat it all out
Those bedroom eyes and them baby pouts
You sweat it all out
Sweat it all out
Sweat it all out
You sweat it all out
Our electric storms and our shifting sands
The candy jars and our sticky hands
Sweat it all out
Sweat it all out
Sweat it all out
You sweat it all out
Now don't forget what I wrote you
Don't forget what I told you
Don't forget that I meant it
When I said
Don't forget your ventolin.

Ernst Moerman (1897 – 1944)

Louis Armstrو

(translated from the french by Samuel Becke

suddenly in the midst of a game of lotto with his sisters
Armstrong let a roar out of him that he had the raw meat
red wet flesh for Louis
and he up and he sliced him two rumplips
since when his trumpet bubbles
their fust buss

poppies burn on the black earth
he weds the floor he lulls her

some of these days muffled in ooze
down down down down
pang of white in my hair

after you've gone
Narcissus lean and slippered

you're driving me crazy and the trumpet
is Ole Bull it chassés aghast
out of the throes of morning

down the giddy catgut
and *confessing* and my woe slavers
the black music it can't be easy
it threshes the old heart into a spin
into a blaze

Louis lil' ole fader Mississippi
his voice gushes into the lake
the rain spouts back into heaven
his arrows from afar they fizz through the wild horses
they fang you and me
then they fly home

flurry of lightning in the earth
sockets for his rootbound song
nights of Harlem scored with his nails
snow black slush when his heart rises

his she-notes they have more tentacles than the sea
they woo me they close my eyes
they suck me out of the world

from Nine Ways of Looking at Ted Hughes

Poet at Work

There he stands
a grizzly bear in a waterfall
catching the leaping salmon
in his scoopy paws

Full Moon and Little Frieda

little Frieda's life
will always be lit by that poem
and so will the life of the moon

Not Cricket

Ted backsomersaulted to catch the meteorite lefthanded.
Rubbed it thoughtfully on the green groin of his flannels
And span it through the ribcage of the Reaper,
Whose bails caught fire

And jumped around the pitch like fire-crackers.
Said the commentator:
Yes Fred, it might have been a meteor –
Could have been a metaphor.

(These were written while Ted was alive to celebrate his work and make him smile that wonderful, lop-sided smile)

Out of Focus

When you take a photograph of Ted
It's a job to get him all in –
like taking a snapshot of Mount Everest

Ted-Watching

I saw him in his apeskin coracle
On the Palaeolithic Swamp
He was chanting in a voice like limestone
To the rhythm of a dinosaur stomp

Then I saw him stalking barefoot
Over hills of stabbing gorse
And I knew he would never stop travelling
Till he reached the river's source

Next I saw him riding a mammoth
Near the banks of the holy stream
And I saw them stop to swim in a pool
Where silver birches dream

And the last I saw was his silhouette
Black against the Northern Lights
So I guess he's up there with the eagles
Who circle the golden heights.

Now the Pterodactyls may mock him
As he howls a prehistoric blues
But we know that he's a marvellous animal
And a great poet – Ted Hughes.

Moondog

There was a man called Moondog
Who made tunes
With thimbles, glasses, zithers,
Keys and spoons
And all the tunes he made
Were living things
Which flew around his head
On silver wings

I bought a Moondog record
Fourteen tracks
A red and golden label
Dusty wax
The sounds were delicate
As cowrie shells
The moonlit dancing
Of a thousand bells

My first day in New York
I walked downtown
Moondog sat on the sidewalk
All in brown
He played his instruments
So sweet and wild
I wanted to stay with him
As his child

Bass voice 1
1. entry

All Is Loneliness

The Freud's Prayer

Our Freud who art in Highgate
Guilt Complex be thy name.
Thy Orgasm come
In life as it does in dreams.
Give us this day our daily Neuroses,
But forgive us our Sadism
As we forgive others their Masochism towards us.
Lead us not into Incest.
But deliver us from Sublimation.
For thine is the Ego, the Id and the Libido
For ever and ever Amen.

Love Affair

He is looking for a Mother
So he can come to rest
On her indulgent breast.

She sees him in his ardour –
He's the Father she never had
Who will be sane when she is mad.

When they wake in mid-storm
Imprisoned in bars of water
Who can comfort the Son and who the Daughter?

POP HEART

"A glass of cider and a chatting-up
and she's yours for life."
Then the Worthington gurgled down the drain
in his face as he leaned against the eternal sunset
of the jukebox which sang:

'Anyone who had a heart would love me.'

"She's a hard girl to drop.
Tries to phone up the wife."
Wheel him into the corner. Tell the girls
he's 'out-of-order'.
I'd rather be wronged by the warm-blooded jukebox
            which sang:

'I was born to love you and shall never be free.'

Grace Nichols

My Northern-Sister

*(for the Finnish-Swedish poet, Edith Södergran, 1892-1923: who
kept faith in her words despite the critics)*

Refusing the crown that would wreathe her as dumb,
my Northern-Sister comes, saying, 'It does not
become me to make myself less than I am.'

And she moves into forest
and she brings me out handfuls of snow,
a rugged fir,
a taste of wild thyme,
which is only a taste of her own joyousness-
the fearless gates she keeps open,
including the one for death.

And she gives me heather and pine,
a taste of blue air,
the talking-memory of my own childhood trees,

Weaving a tender chemistry with her red
red heart.

And what have I got to give her?
Only the little thing she says
she's always wanted-
a small letter, to be read on a garden bench
with a cat in the sun.

Edith, my sister, come and sit down.

Abra-Cadabra

My mother had more magic
in her thumb
than the length and breadth
of any magician

Weaving incredible stories
around the dark-green senna brew
just make us slake
the ritual Sunday purgative

Knowing when to place a cochineal poultice
on a fevered forehead
Knowing how to measure a belly's symmetry
kneading the narah pains away

Once my baby sister stuffed
a split-pea up her nostril
my mother got a crochet needle
and gently tried to pry it out

We stood around her
like inquisitive gauldings

Suddenly, in surgeon's tone she ordered,
'Pass the black pepper,'
and patted a little
under the dozing nose

My baby sister sneezed.
The rest was history.

Blake's purest daughter

'All things pass,
Love and mankind is glass'
— Stevie Smith

Must she always walk with death, must she?
I went out and asked the sky.
No, it said, no,
She'll do as I do, as I do.
I go on forever.

Must she always walk with Death, must she?
I went and asked the soil.
No, it said, no,
She'll do as I do, as I do.
I will nourish her forever.

Must she always walk with Death, must she?
I listened to the water.
No, it said, no.
She'll do as I do, as I do.
I will cleanse her forever.

Must she always walk with Death, must she?
No, said the fire.
She'll burn as I burn, as I burn.
She will be in brilliance forever.

O but I am not Death, said Death slyly,
I am only no longer living,
Only no longer knowing exorbitant grief.
Do not fear me, so many share me.

Stevie elemental
Free now of the personal,
Through sky and soil
And fire and water
Swim on. Blake's purest daughter!

Harvest of learning I have reaped,
Fruits of many a lifetime stored,
The false discarded, proven kept,
Knowledge that is its own reward,
　　　No written page more true
　　　Than blade of grass and drop of dew.

Striven my partial self to bind
Within tradition great and whole,
Christendom's two thousand years,
Wisdom's universal mind.
　　　No doctrine heart can heal
　　　As cloudless sky and lonely hill.

Now I am old my books I close
And forget religion's ties,
Untrammelled the departing soul
Puts out of mind both false and true,
　　　Distant hills and spacious skies,
　　　Grass-blade and morning dew.

What are those golden builders doing?
for Frances and Michael Horovitz

O lovely mild Jerusalem
Whose hope is like a memory,
Are you a city or a dream,
Or in your always coming down
From heaven to earth, from thought to form
Transient as music in the air
Where we may set no foot upon
Towers and arches built of sound,
Intangible as heart's desire?

Descending angels in a dream
Inspire the plan the dreamer lays
With square and compass on the floor,
But visions out of time and space
Returning, carry soon away:
Yet here or there the temple shines,
Its seven lamps with tongues of flame
Encircle and illuminate
Sanctuaries of exiled men.

In England's gray polluted land
our cities are not built of gold,
But ground-plan, sketch, or little phrase
Is there, one evening, in some house
Of friendship, music, or of books,
In cloister, garden, concert-hall
Some detail of the master-plan,
Tomorrow lost, is found today,
And memory is like a hope
As we repair, remake, build on.

Ifigenija Simonovic *(translated by Anthony Rudolf and the author)*

Nights Are Dark

Nights dark. Nights long.
Nights full of stars, like lonely canopies.
I am warming up. I am softening.

Hands cold. Hands dry.
Hands awkward. Like my mouth.
Coming closer. Softening.

Words inward. Words enclosed.
Silence warm. Like thoughts.
Stopping half way. soft.

Your skin smooth. Calm.
Only breath says you're alive. Like memory.
You're a wave. I'm your cliff. Still.

Two Stages

I am silent
      What is the matter
Nothing
I hope I will not start shouting

I am shouting
      What is the matter
Nothing
I hope I will not become silent

Little Boat Floating

spring comes
        without fail ever

willow trees green
        whilst I hesitate
        (do I want more springs?)
a bird floats its song
        on the air – it
        doesn't ask why waters
        overflow why they
        run blindly why
ice eats into valleys

                go on floating
                go on floating

spring throws mud in our eyes
awakens us with sunrays
        then strikes us blind
– nothing that runs
        or flies or crawls
        can escape ever

peasants cut down trees
birdsong falls off

                go on floating
                go on floating

My Muse

My Muse sits forlorn
She wishes she had not been born
She sits in the cold
No word she says is ever told.

Why does my Muse only speak when she is unhappy?
She does not, I only listen when I am unhappy
When I am happy I live and despise writing
For my Muse this cannot but be dispiriting.

Words

Why do people abuse so much our busy age?
They can withdraw into themselves and not rage
It is better to do this and live in one's own kingdom
Than by raging add to the rage of our busy time.

This is an age when there are too many words
Silent silent silent the waters lie
And the beautiful grass lies silent and this is beautiful
Why can men then not withdraw and be silent and happy?

It is better to see the grass than write about it
Better to see the water than write a water song
Yet both may be painted and a person be happy in the painting
Can it be that the tongue is cursed, to go so wrong?

From my diary

"She was," my father said (in an aside)
"A great beauty, forty years ago."
Out of my crude childhood, I stared at
Our hostess, tremulous
In her armchair, pouring tea from silver –
Her mauve flowered dress, her grey sad gaze.
I only saw her being seventy
I did not see the girl my father saw.

Now that I'm older than my father then was
I go with life-long friends to the same parties
That we have gone to always.
We seem the same age always
Although the parties sometimes change to funerals
That sometimes used to change to christenings.

Faces we've once loved
Fit into their seven ages as Russian dolls
Fit into one another.
My memory penetrates through successive layers
Back to you when I saw you first... So when the last
Exterior image is laid under it's lid
Your face first seen will glow through all.

Wuxi – Shanghai Express

A girl who has drowned herself speaks:

"If only they hadn't shown that cruel mercy
Of dredging my drowned body from the river
That locked me in it's peace, up to their surface
Of autopsy, and burial, and forms –
That, which was my last wish, might have come true: –
When the waves had finally washed away
The tatters of my flesh, the skull would stay
But change to crystal: things outside
Which it had looked at once, would swim into
Eye-sockets that looked at them: through
The scooped-out hollows of the skull would dart
Solid phosphorescent fish, where there had been
Images of them only, in the brain."

"GHETTO DEFENDANT"

This is from the 1982 Clash LP Combat Rock. Allen Ginsberg and Peter Orlovsky had taken to hanging out at the sessions. Finally one night, after cutting the vocal on this tune, I walked back into the control booth and said:
"We've got America's Greatest Living Poet sitting here, c'mon Allen, what about getting on the track?"
He replied, unexpectedly:
"What do you want me to sound like?"
I thought for a moment and said:
"er . . . The Voice of God . . . er . . . rapping . . ."
He took off his glasses:
"So, you want me to sound like what The Voice of God would sound like, if God were rapping?"
"Yes" I replied. In the silence that followed, Orlovsky's voice came cutting in loud and clear from the back of the couch:
"Jeez!!! You pushy limeys don't want much, do ya?"

As you can hear on the record, in the stereo split, Allen is on the left side, intoning, and I'm panned to the other. I've tried to space it to show where he placed his vocal in the song.
A moody reggae track begins.
Soon the "Voice of God" is heard, musing down from the mountain.

Ginsberg: This side, rapping   Strummer: This side singing

STARVED IN METROPOLIS, HOOKED ON NECROPOLIS,
ADDICT OF METROPOLIS, DO THE WORM ON ACROPOLIS,
SLAM DANCE THE COSMOPOLIS, ENLIGHTEN THE POPULACE...

                    HUNGRY DARKNESS OF LIVING,
                    WHO WILL THIRST IN THE PIT?

...HOOKED ON NECROPOLIS...   SHE SPENT A LIFETIME DECIDING,
                    HOW TO RUN FROM IT.

...ADDICT OF METROPOLIS...   ONCE FATE HAD A WITNESS,
                    AND THE YEARS SEEMED LIKE FRIENDS,

...GIRLFRIENDS...
                    NOW A GIRL HAS A DREAM,

...SHOT IN ETERNITY...
                    BUT IT BEGINS LIKE IT ENDS,

...METHADONE KITTY...   GHETTO DEFENDANT!

...IRON SERENITY...   IT IS HEROIN PITY,
                    NOT TEAR GAS NOR BATON CHARGE,
                        THAT STOPS YOU TAKING THE CITY.

...STRUNG OUT COMMITTEE...
                    WALLED OUT OF THE CITY,
                    CLUBBED DOWN FROM UPTOWN,
                    SPRAYED PEST FROM THE NEST,

...THE GUARDS ARE ITCHY...   RUN OUT TO BARRIO TOWN,
                    FORCED TO WATCH AT THE FEAST,
                    GHETTO DEFENDANT!

...STRUNG OUT COMMITTEE...
                    IT IS HEROIN PITY,
...NOT SITTING PRETTY...   NOT TEAR GAS NOR BATON CHARGE,
                    WILL STOP YOU TAKING THE CITY

...AFGHANISTAN, MEDITATION,
OLD CHINESE FLU, KICK JUNK,
WHAT ELSE CAN A POOR WORKER DO?

Eric "J" Thribb (17½)

In Memoriam William Burroughs, Great American Writer

So Farewell
Then
William S.
Burroughs

"The Naked Lunch"
Yes
That was your
Masterpiece.

Keith thought it
Was a cookbook
For nudists

And gave it
To his Auntie.

But she said
She could
Not get the
Hang of

The recipes.

(P.S. this poem was written under the influence of a hallucinatory salmon and shrimp sandwich and strikes me as the most brilliant one I have written in my entire life)

The following poem was written specially for Radio 4 as part of its celebration of National Poetry Day and recited by the author:

The Six Pips

P i p
P i p
P i p
P i p
P i p
P e e p

The six Pips
Yes. We
Hear them
Every day.

But what
Are they ?

And why
Are there
Six ?

And why is the sixth
One longer
Than the others ?

It is a
Mystery

The following two pages reproduce an excerpt from the score of Stan Tracey's 'Jazz Suite inspired by Dylan Thomas's *Under Milk Wood*' (– this section evokes the reminiscent dreaming of Captain Cat)

PIANO

I LOST MY STEP IN NANTUCKET

INTO BLOWING. REGULAR BLUES CHANGES

from **Bone Girl**

. . . Bones jut through the skin, raising desire, asking to be
touched.
A finger traces a curve, an outline, a knot.
Shadows.
The hard of bone. Soft of skin.

Bones - bare and to the point.
Brittle when the sun doesn't shine.

. . . . famine again
mothers
children
      all
         bones
              dead almost
      will not let go
         birth pangs
never die

. . . He is speaking, his tallness hooked
with age. Cheekbones, scarcely
fleshed, pocket his eyes.
Lips balance
on the bone of his face.

He looks as he lived.

"If I can be useful," he says
"Use me."

Ilse Elise, Julie Judith, Michael, Leo, Felix and Joseph Horovitz in the garden of 30 Obermain Anlage, Frankfurt, early in 1937, photographed by Recha Kollin.

in memoriam Rosi Reline Horovitz
née Feist (23rd October 1894 – 27th May 1995)

Michael Horovitz

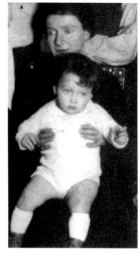

(M H on Rosi's lap, 1937)

from GROWING UP

. . . all alone in the shop
i am five years old

the moon is bright
the leaves bright green

birds are sleeping
the air is quiet

quietly the curtain waves
the boats sailing out to sea

in an early morning the
wind blowing billowing hard

the ship is big and the
books are good and

stories are told but . . . Oh
Great! – here's Mummy

– yesterday she went away
and it was hard to take

her place

Mother

By candlelight, at ninety-six
She looks inside her mind
Hard, seeking each child
She brought into a shaky world
Three cut off
At birth, six, fifty
Some who revolve in her orbit, slowly
Others flown out and away.
Her gaze fastens on each in turn
Wondering why and where
They are battered, suffering
And also glowing, singing
Joined to her
By fine unbreakable threads
She prays for them
And for her own uncertain fate.

August 1991

(M H and R H, early 1970s)

April 1995 (Mum's last Pesach)

Visited Mum at Goldstar Old People's Home. Now that she's 100 and 7 months, she's decided to stay in there just for the Passover week. When I came in through the main entrance off Platts Lane, an old woman in a crumpled white muslin dressing gown seemed to be straining at the end of a string, like a dog tethered to its kennel.

    The receptionist, Mrs. Kaplan, said I'd find Mummy in the Sun Lounge. I was ushered through a long room whose walls were lined with chairs all round, oldies sat in most of them, several muttering to themselves, one wrestling with an invisible adversary. A giant TV set was the centrepiece of one wall. Most of the occupants were women ("Widows like me", Mum said later).

    On passing into the adjoining room, my heart leapt up to see her in the corner, almost the only person in the crowded sunlit glasshouse area involved in a dialogue with the others. Though the tiniest of them, she was as so often standing up tremendously straight, with at least four or five others around her, reminding me of the most popular child in the school playground, in whose halo or aura others circled, keeping a reverent space between them and her. It took her a minute to realise who I was, and then her first concern was to try to introduce me to her group – but though she knew all their names, most of them seemed way beyond comprehending or carrying through such a formality. Then Mum suggested we go to her room, found her stick and hobbled in front, guiding me to the lift. We went to her room on the top floor, which overlooks Finchley Road at its busiest intersection between Hampstead and Golders Green.

    She asked me to close the window, and we sat and looked at one another. I was overwhelmed: it was the first time I'd seen her to sit down with and look at, alone, outside her house, for many years. I tried to stop myself from weeping, and she seemed not to notice. She spoke, with her customary measured gentleness and precision, of the new routines in the Home, of how everything was done for her, which made her "get lazy".

Michael Horovitz

(Sketch of R H by M H. 1987)

It was as though many years of our relationship (60 this year) were peeled away. My eyes had difficulty in sustaining the meeting her upright steady gaze tacitly solicited, but just about managed, especially when she got talking again. Just one of the very few elderly men there apparently likes to sing, and speak of, her beloved Jewish hymns and prayers before, during and after meals.

We slowly went downstairs again, and passed through the main sitting room to go out for a brief but leisurely walk. The inmates were sat uneasily, looking sharply away from one another or at their feet, which were variously shod, slippered or bare. Most clutched into themselves like nervous, shy infants left to get on with it on their own at a party where they hardly knew any of the others, nor wanted to.

The man Mum sang with at meals waved to her amiably, reminding me of the story George Melly tells about a bloke at an Old Folks Home get-together who buttonholes the biddy he fancies with the gambit: "I bet you don't know my name, do you?" "Naw I dawn't", she replies, in a Northern accent, "but if you ask Matron, I'm sure she'll be able to tell it you".

Mum looked at everything outside with her wonted avid curiosity. Whenever she wanted to speak she halted, and fixed her bright sky-blue eyes on me. I tried to keep hold of her hand, but every moment she felt able to walk alone, she would grasp her stick fiercely and do so.

It was a dazzling spring day; suddenly we found ourselves on Kidderpore Avenue suffused in white, pink and gold light streaming down through the flocculent blossoms heaving and shimmering on a clump of high trees back from the road. Mum immediately stepped under them, inhaled deeply, and said the blessing for first sight of blossoms this year. Then turned to go back to the Goldstar.

She placed the warm cask of her tender hands round my bowed head, as she always did when we were about to part, and quietly blessed me. We kissed on each cheek at the Home's entrance, and I watched her go in to join the end of the long slowly lurching procession to lunch.

123

(from left to right: Ilse Elise, Leo, Selma, Rosi, Felix, Marcus, Abraham, Michael, Auguste, Joseph, Martin, Judith, circa 1936 – about a year before the family fled from Frankfurt to London)

(from left to right: Selma, Michael, Martin, Aba, Roberta Benjamin [Selma and Alfred's elder daughter], Felix, Rosi, Elsie – as she had become renamed long before 1946, when this photo was taken by Alfred Benjamin)

Royal Free Hospital
26·5·95
bed (10.30 pm
(had died
9·30 a.m.)

George & Mary ward
Royal Free Hospital
26 May '95

Rosi
11 – 11.15 27 May
died about
8 a m

Adam Horovitz

In Memory

These broken voices,
　　　　splintered eyes,
　　　　bend like the boughs of hollow trees
　　　　in supplication and in grief.

They stay motionless
　　　　while the bodies rise
　　　　to wash their hands
　　　　before they eat

and from their lips
　　　　the Kaddish sighs.
　　　　Swift and silent
　　　　as owls they pray.

Then even the care-worn voices
　　　　are caught in song,
　　　　in lush melody. In memory
　　　　of the calm one who has passed away.

And all that tears can do
　　　　is wash out pain.
　　　　The salt still falls onto the bread.
　　　　They are bound by DNA

　　　　　　　to their mother's love,
　　　　　　　for she exists in all of them

and in the lives they've led.

(from left to right: Martin, Selma, Marcus, Rosi, Leo, Gustel [aka Orah – thus renamed when she settled in Israel in 1952], Michael, Elise [as she had re-renamed herself since moving to Paris in 1958].
This photo was taken in Mummy's front room, circa 1994 by Alfred Benjamin)

(from left to right: Rosi, Adam, Michael and Selma photographed in the same room by Alfred, circa 1993)

For my Mother
(Rosi Horovitz, 1894 – 1995)

She's returned now
to the cosmic cycle
that gave her a moment in time
one hundred years
enough to give us life
joy and tears
someone to think and care about
as she thought and cared about us
her little kitchen our meeting-place.

She gave us
what she missed
a mother's love
a mother's blessings
right into our own old age
her mind stayed close
to each of us
even after her body
could no longer handle
the rolling stairs, buses
trains and airplanes
to bring her to us.

I think of her now
as a star with a steadfast light
a granite rock in sun and rain
until she comes back
in another delightful
human form.

Farewell, sweet Mother!